Annual Snowpack Report 2011-2012

Central Alaska Network

Natural Resource Data Series NPS/CAKN/NRDS—2013/424

Pamela J. Sousanes

National Park Service
4175 Geist Road
Fairbanks, AK 99709

January 2013

U.S. Department of the Interior
National Park Service
Natural Resource Stewardship and Science
Fort Collins, Colorado

The National Park Service, Natural Resource Stewardship and Science office in Fort Collins, Colorado publishes a range of reports that address natural resource topics of interest and applicability to a broad audience in the National Park Service and others in natural resource management, including scientists, conservation and environmental constituencies, and the public.

The Natural Resource Data Series is intended for the timely release of basic data sets and data summaries. Care has been taken to assure accuracy of raw data values, but a thorough analysis and interpretation of the data has not been completed. Consequently, the initial analyses of data in this report are provisional and subject to change.

All manuscripts in the series receive the appropriate level of peer review to ensure that the information is scientifically credible, technically accurate, appropriately written for the intended audience, and designed and published in a professional manner. Data in this report were collected and analyzed using methods based on established, peer-reviewed protocols and were analyzed and interpreted within the guidelines of the protocols.

Views, statements, findings, conclusions, recommendations, and data in this report do not necessarily reflect views and policies of the National Park Service, U.S. Department of the Interior. Mention of trade names or commercial products does not constitute endorsement or recommendation for use by the U.S. Government.

This report is available from the Central Alaska Network website (http://www.nature.nps.gov/im/units/cakn) and the Natural Resource Publications Management website (http://www.nature.nps.gov/publications/nrpm).

Please cite this publication as:

Sousanes, P.J. 2013. Annual snowpack report 2011-2012: Central Alaska Network. Natural Resource Data Series NPS/CAKN/NRDS—2013/424. National Park Service, Fort Collins, Colorado.

NPS 953/119555, January 2013

Contents

Figures

Executive Summary

Statewide snowfall totals were variable for 2011-2012 with much of the attention focused on the south central and south east regions of Alaska where record snowfall totals were recorded. Snowfall totals were also above normal in the west and northwest areas of the state. The Central Alaska Network (CAKN) region had a variable snowpack that ranged from well above normal along the southern coast of Wrangell –St. Elias National Park and Preserve, to above normal south of the Alaska Range and in the western areas of Denali NP&P, to near normal in Yukon Charley, and just below normal in the central region (the eastern/central regions of Denali). The first persistent snowpack arrived around the week of October 16. The snowpack persisted into May at most sites in the CAKN region, with a few exceptions. Snow off dates were recorded at May Creek on April 27, followed by Kantishna on May 7, Chisana on May 9, American Creek on May 12, and Tokositna on May 27.

Acknowledgments

The data and results in this report would not be possible without the help of a number of people. Thanks to Miranda Terwilliger for helping coordinate the surveys in Wrangell-St. Elias National Park. Thank you to Paul Atkinson for doing the snow surveys for Yukon-Charley National Preserve, to Mike Thompson and Pete Dalton for doing surveys in Wrangell-St. Elias National Park and Preserve. And, many thanks to the park pilots, Colin Milone and Peter Christian and Arctic Air Alaska pilot/owner Sandy Hamilton, for flying safely and getting field data during the coldest and darkest time of the year. I also would like to thank Rick McClure, Dan Kenny, and Daniel Fisher from NRCS, who make the surveys and data dissemination seamless.

Introduction and Methods

Denali National Park and Preserve, Wrangell –St. Elias National Park and Preserve, and Yukon-Charley Rivers National Preserve make up the Central Alaska Inventory and Monitoring Network (CAKN) covering over 21 million acres. The network was established to monitor key components of ecosystems in the three parks and to provide that information back to park managers for use in the stewardship of natural resources. A predominate feature of climate in high latitude regions is the presence of a seasonal snowpack. The snow cover protects and insulates the ground and low-lying plants, reduces desiccation, and maintains ground temperatures near the freezing level. This seasonal snow cover, lasting up to eight months out of the year, is an important ecological factor for subarctic park ecosystems. A main objective of the CAKN snowpack monitoring program is to record long-term trends in snow and monitor changes in the extent, duration, and character of the seasonal snow cover. This is accomplished through an interagency agreement with the Natural Resources Conservation Service (NRCS) to survey snow courses and aerial snow markers and to install and maintain Snow Telemetry (SNOTEL) sites in all three CAKN parks. The SNOTEL sites have proven to be the most accurate instrumented sites to document all forms of precipitation in Alaska, including snowfall which is difficult to measure in remote locations. The agreement between the NPS and NRCS includes data dissemination and archiving. These summary reports compile snowpack data for the central Alaska region and are produced annually. The timing of the report follows the end of the water year which runs from October 1 through September 30. The data provided in this report comes almost exclusively from the NRCS Alaska Snow, Water and Climate Services web based server (NRCS 2012).

Snow pack is measured in several different ways in the Central Alaska Network. A brief description of the survey methods and data collection follows. For detailed methods refer to the Snowpack Monitoring Protocols for the CAKN (Sousanes, 2006).

SNOTEL

The most useful information available on snow pack is from the new CAKN automated SNOw TELemetry (SNOTEL) sites at Kantishna and Tokositna Valley in Denali National Park and Preserve and at May Creek and Chisana in Wrangell – St. Elias National Park and Preserve. . Each SNOTEL site has a year round precipitation gauge that measures snow and rain along with a meteorological station that records air temperature, solar radiation, summer rainfall, and snow depth. Most SNOTEL sites also have a pressure sensing snow pillow that records the density of the snowpack. The data are recorded and transmitted hourly from these sites. SNOTEL sites adjacent to CAKN parks are also useful, including the new American Creek site at Eagle near Yukon-Charley Rivers National Preserve, and the Upper Tsaina SNOTEL south of Copper Center near Wrangell – St. Elias National Park and Preserve.

Snow Courses and Aerial Markers

There are 20 snow courses and aerial snow markers in the three CAKN parks (Figure 1). Park staff, including park pilots, as well as contract pilots fly these surveys the last 3 days of each month from November through April. A certain amount of logistic flexibility and cold weather hardiness is necessary to undertake these surveys. Weather and daylight are critical factors in making sure they are done safely.

Snow Depth Sensors

Acoustic snow depth sensors were added to most of the CAKN and Remote Automated Weather Station (RAWS) climate stations that were installed in the past few years. This measurement offers a cumulative look at snowpack development through the season.

National Weather Service Sites

The McKinley Park, Eagle, Cantwell, McCarthy, and Yakutat National Weather Service Cooperative Observer sites, or COOP sites, manually record snow depth and precipitation on a daily basis. These sites have records dating back many decades and are valuable for long term trend analysis.

  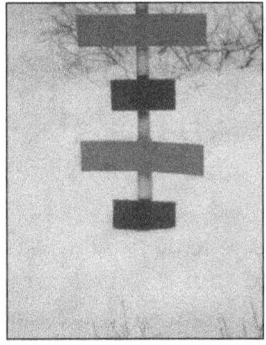

Figure 1. Example of a snow course (left), SNOTEL (center), and aerial snow marker (right).

Snow surveys in all three CAKN parks are done on Dec 1, Feb 1, March 1, April 1 and May 1, if weather conditions permit. The snow monitoring sites for the CAKN are shown in Figure 2. Data are available on the NRCS website at http://www.ak.nrcs.usda.gov/snow/; the sites specific to the Central Alaska region are compiled in this report.

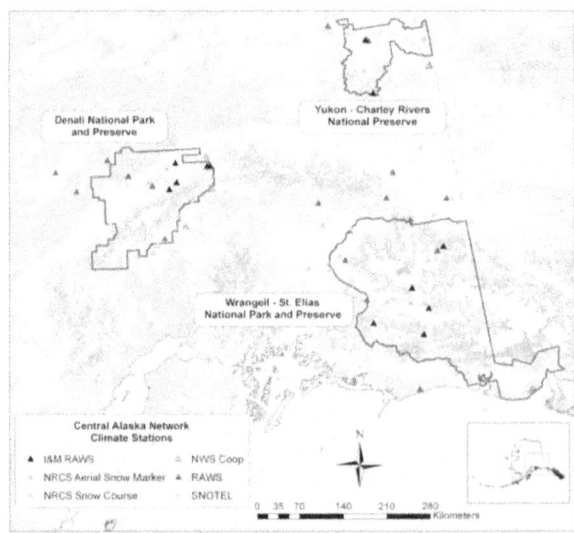

Figure 2. Locations of snow monitoring sites in the Central Alaska Network.

Results

The CAKN region had a variable snowpack that ranged from well above normal along the southern coast of Wrangell –St. Elias NP&P, to above normal south of the Alaska Range and in the western areas of Denali NP&P, to near normal in Yukon Charley, and just below normal in the central region (the eastern/central regions of Denali). The first persistent snowpack arrived around the week of October 16th. In Denali, both the Kantishna and Tokositna Valley snowpack started on October 16th. The May Creek SNOTEL in Wrangell-St. Elias recorded the first persistent snowpack on October 18th, while the Chisana site on the north side of the park started earlier on October 8th. The snowpack persisted into May at all of the CAKN SNOTEL sites except for May Creek; snow off occurred at May Creek on April 27th, followed by Kantishna on May 7th, Chisana on May 9th, American Creek on May 12, and Tokositna on May 27th.

Air temperatures around the region varied tremendously in 2011-2012; every month there were average temperature departures from normal in the opposite direction. October temperatures were warmer than normal around the CAKN region, November temperatures were well below normal; December temperatures were well above normal. The month of January was frigid statewide, particularly north and west of the Alaska Range. February temperatures continued the trend with warmer than normal temperatures, March swung back the opposite direction and had temperatures that were well-below normal, and April ended the snow season with temperatures that were much warmer than normal. The following sections provides a summary of the snowpack season for each of the major hydrologic units in the central Alaska region including the Central Yukon Basin, Tanana Basin, Western Interior Basin, Copper River Basin, and the Matanuska-Susitna Basin (Figure 3).

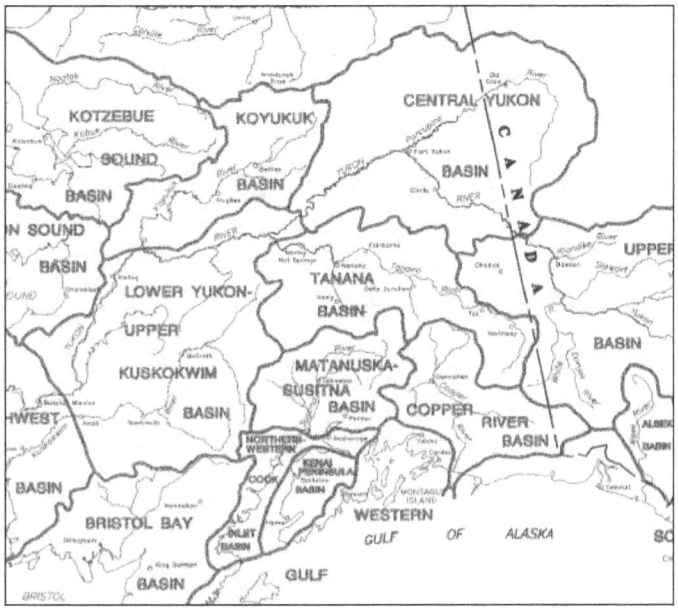

Figure 3. Map showing USGS hydrologic basins of Alaska. Map courtesy of the Natural Resources Conservation Service (NRCS, 2011) and available at http://ambcs.org/pub/BasinRpt/2011/may.pdf.

Central Yukon Basin

Yukon-Charley Rivers lies within the Central Yukon Basin. This region had below normal conditions in the early season and transitioned to a near normal snowpack with significant snowfall in December. The Coal Creek climate station reported the first measurable snow on October 18, 2011. The long term cooperative weather station at Eagle reported a total of 5.5 inches of snow for October when the normal is 9.6 inches. In November, Eagle had 7 inches of snow for the month – still below the average of 10.6 inches. The December snowfall total for Eagle was 17.9 inches, well above the 11.3 inch average for the month. There was no snow survey done on December 1 due to weather conditions at the airstrip. The aerial markers throughout the Preserve had between 7 and 17 inches of snow for the early season measurements.

Throughout December and early January the snow continued to fall, the surveys were not done in the Preserve on February 1 due to poor flying conditions, but other sites in the area reported near normal snow depths for the month. The snowfall total for February was above normal for Eagle with 7.7 inches falling during the month. The snow depths around the Preserve on March 1 were lowest in the central region near Copper Creek and Crescent Creek where 13 and 18 inches of snow were measured. The Upper Charley River basin had 27 inches of snow and the sites north of the Yukon River had between 28 and 30 inches of snow. The Coal Creek snow course had 20 inches on March 1. The temperatures in March were cold and there was little additional snowfall for the month, the measurements for the April 1 survey were nearly the same as the March 1 surveys.

There was still measureable snow at most sites around the Preserve on May 1, and the average for the region was just above normal for this time of year. The American Creek SNOTEL site at Eagle had 8 inches of snow on the first of the month and an aerial wolf monitoring survey noted an estimated 2 to 3 inches of snow cover around the Preserve around May 1. The graphs taken from the NRCS Alaska Snow Survey Report for May 1 show the average of all of the snow courses within the watershed with temperatures from a nearby long-running climate station (Figure 4).

The new American Creek SNOTEL site was installed in summer of 2011. There was a total of 4.0 inches of precipitation accumulated from October 1 through May. The Eagle NWS COOP site recorded an annual snowfall amount of 62.0 inches or 103% of the normal 59.9 inches. See Appendix C for tables and graphs with long-term data.

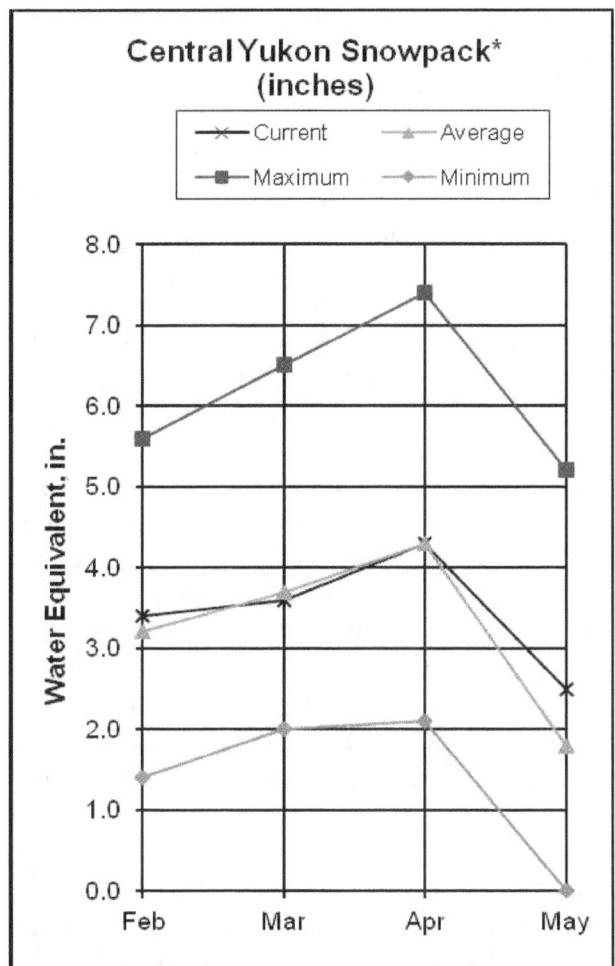

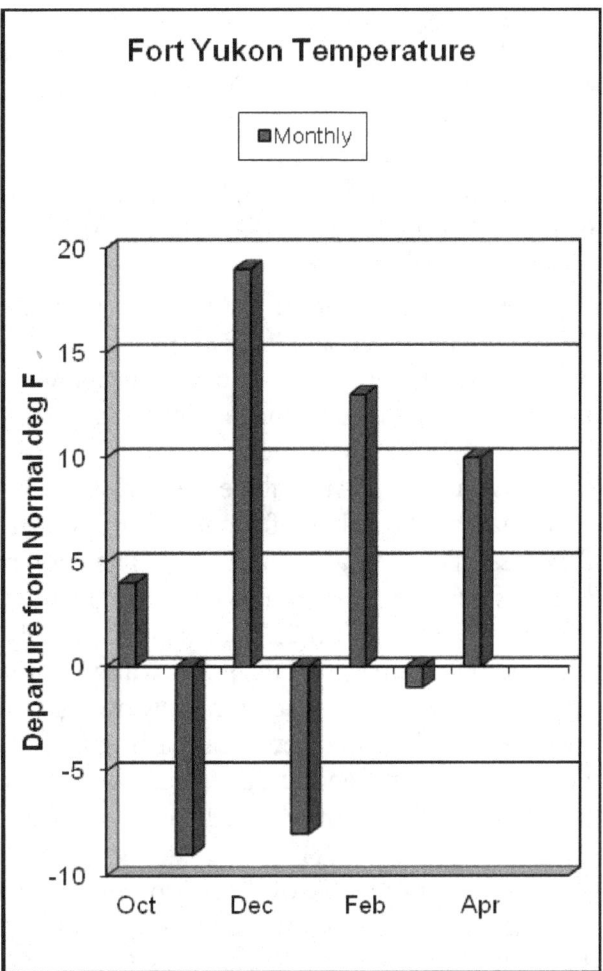

Figure 4. Central Yukon Basin 2011-2012 snow season. Courtesy of NRCS, Anchorage, AK (NRCS, 2012).

Tanana Basin

The park regions that are part of the Tanana Basin hydrologic basin, just north of the Alaska Range, include the north side of Denali from park headquarters to Kantishna and the northern areas of Wrangell - St. Elias from the Canadian border to the northeastern areas of Wrangell – St. Elias, including Chisana. The SNOTEL sites at Kantishna in Denali and Chisana in Wrangell–St. Elias record daily snow depth and precipitation data, which provides the "snow on" date for the seasonal snowpack, after this date snow generally remains on the ground for the rest of the winter. On October 16, Kantishna recorded the first persistent snow of the season and October 8 marked the beginning of the season at Chisana. At the Denali Park headquarters site the day of the first persistent snow was October 17, a few weeks later than normal.

There was little snow accumulation in October, but by November the snowpack was beginning to develop. On December 1 the Kantishna site had 12 inches of snow and Chisana had 14 inches of snow. The Denali Park headquarters site had 8 inches of snow on November 30; the long-term average is 10 inches for this date. Jatahmund Lake, north of Chisana in WRST, reported 12 inches of snow on November 30, which is about 75% of normal. After the first survey of the season, there was considerable snowfall throughout the Tanana Basin in December. The December snowfall total for Denali Park headquarters NWS site was 18 inches, 144% of normal.

On February 1, the snowpack in the western portion of the Tanana Basin was just about normal; Kantishna had 21 inches of snow with a SWE of 4.2 inches, normal is 26 inches of snow with a SWE of 4.5 inches. The middle Tanana Basin snowpack was near normal to above normal, with sites at and around Denali Park headquarters at 110% of normal, with depths ranging from 20 to 23 inches. The snow depth at Chisana was only 75% of normal with 15 inches of snow and a SWE of 2.7 inches. Lost Creek snow course on the Nabesna Road had 13 inches of snow, which is well below the normal 25 inches. The Jatahmund Lake snow course had 15 inches of snow, just below the normal 16 inches of snow.

Through March and April the eastern region had a snowpack that was similar to February. Kantishna had 24 inches of snow and a SWE of 4.7 inches on March 1, normal is 28 inches with 5.3 inches of snow water equivalent. The snowpack remained below normal at Lost Creek with 18 inches of snow. Jatahmund Lake was just below normal for snow depth and snow water content at 17 inches and 2.7 inches, respectively. At Chisana, the snow depth was 18 inches, 2 inches below normal, and the snow water equivalent was 3.0 inches, normal is 3.4 inches. The sites near Denali Park headquarters were again near normal at the Rock Creek sites, to above normal at park headquarters. Lake Minchumina was visited for the March 1 survey and had 22 inches of snow, just above the normal for the month. The snow water equivalent was 3.3 inches, normal is 4.0 inches for March 1.

For the last snow survey of the season the snow depths ranged from 4 inches of snow at Chisana in the eastern region to 5 inches of snow at Kantishna. There was no snow at Lake Minchumina, Jatahmund Lake, and the lower Rock Creek site on May 1. Denali Park headquarters had 7 inches of snow on the ground on May 1, which is just below normal. Figure 5 shows the NRCS snow survey report graphs for the area. See Appendix A for individual site data.

The Kantishna SNOTEL site recorded 5.2 inches of total winter precipitation (snow water equivalent) from October 1, 2011 through May 1, 2012, which is 84% of average. The total annual precipitation for the site was 23.5 inches; the winter snow accounted for 22% the total annual precipitation. Snow-on date was October 16 and the snow-off date was May 7, 2012. The Chisana SNOTEL site recorded 4.1 inches of total winter precipitation from Oct 1 through May 1. The total annual precipitation was 12.3 inches; the winter snow accounted for 33% of the total annual precipitation. The McKinley Park long-term NWS site was 87% of normal for the year with an annual total of 69.5 inches of snow. Snow on date was October 17 and snow off date was May 7, 2012. See Appendix B for snowfall and precipitation accumulation graphs. See Appendix C for tables and graphs with long-term data.

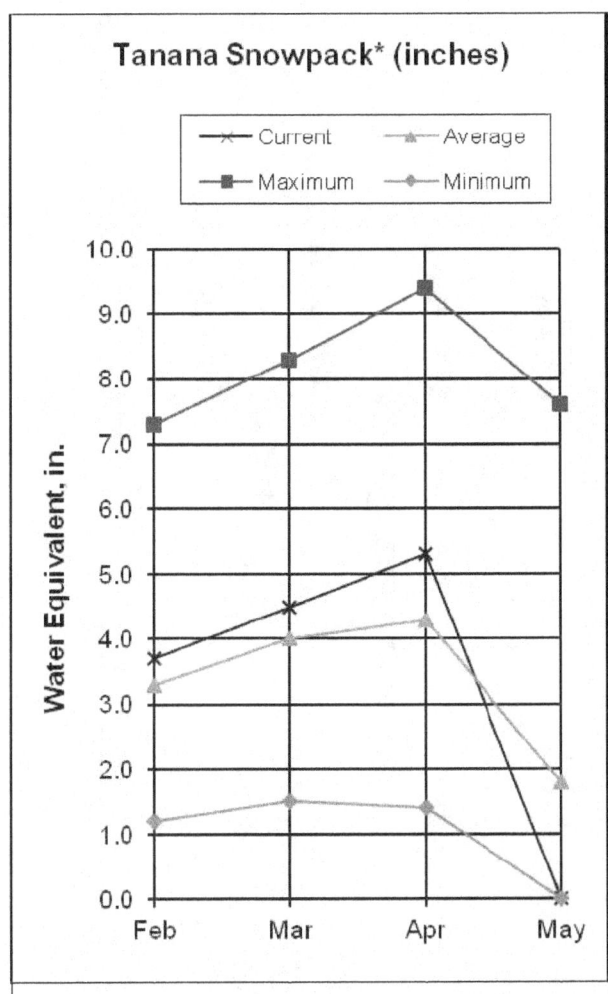
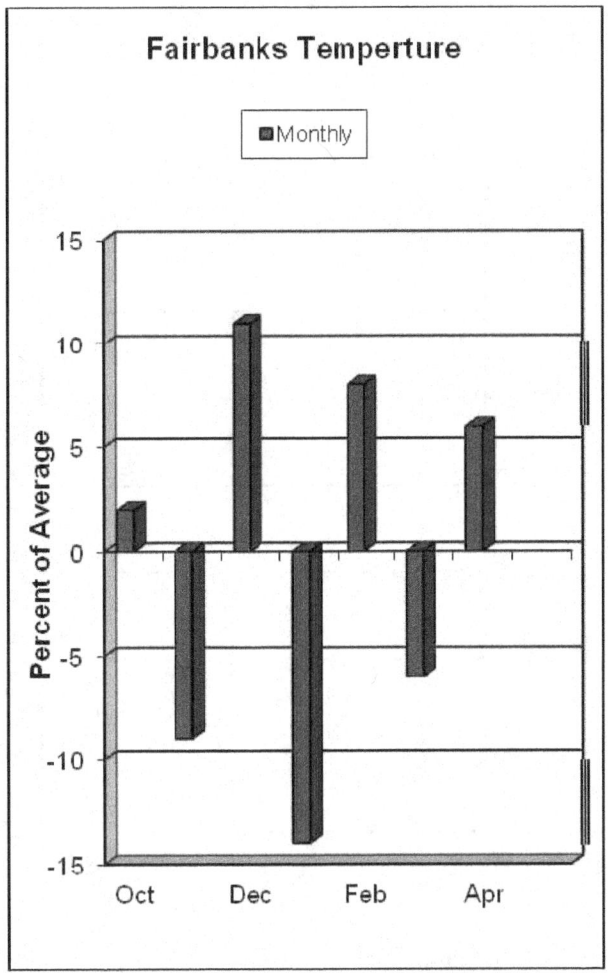

Figure 5. Tanana Basin 2011-2012 snow season. Graphs courtesy of the NRCS, Anchorage, AK (NRCS, 2012).

Western Interior Basin

The northwestern areas of Denali, that include the watersheds that drain west into the Kuskokwim River, are part of the Western Interior Basin hydrologic unit. The Purkeypile site was surveyed on December 1; there was 13 inches of snow and the snow water content was 2.0 inches. By March 1 the site had 26 inches of snow and 5.3 inches of water content, which is 143% of normal. The April snow survey was the last survey of the season and the snowpack was 120% of normal with 23 inches of snow and 6.0 inches of water content. The landing conditions were not good for the May 1 survey; the snow was patchy and there was some snow remaining on the snow course. Figure 6 shows the NRCS snow survey report graphs for the entire Western Interior Basin.

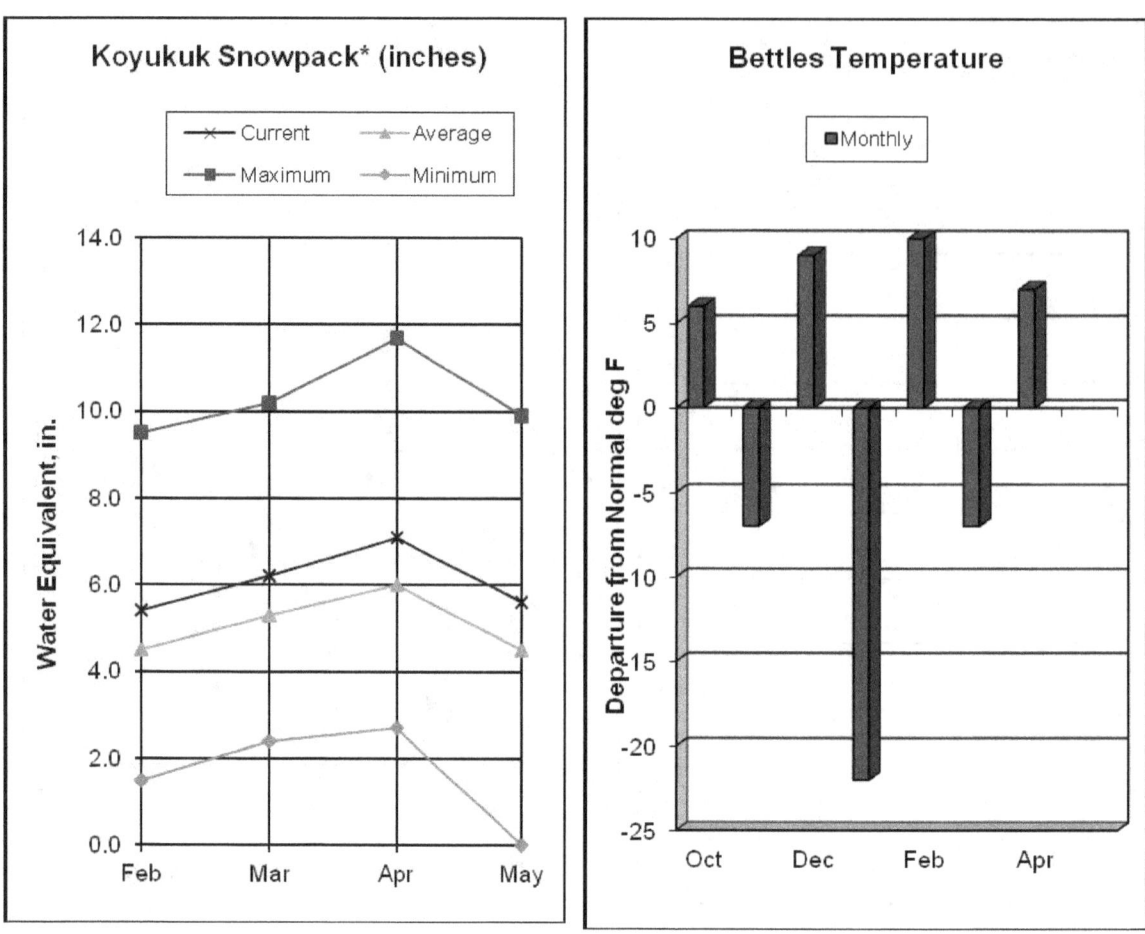

Figure 6. Western Interior (Koyukuk Basin) 2011-2012 snow season. Courtesy of NRCS, Anchorage, AK 2012.

Copper Basin

The Copper Basin is divided into 3 regions that encompass Wrangell – St. Elias: the Chugach Range, the Basin Floor and the Wrangell Mountains. There are two SNOTEL sites in the park, one at May Creek on the Basin Floor, and one at Chisana. The Chisana data is included in the Tanana Basin hydrologic unit. The May Creek SNOTEL recorded the first persistent snow on October 18, 2011 and the snowpack steadily increased throughout the snow season. On December 1st there was 12 inches of snow with a water content of 1.4 inches, normal for that time of year, but the water content was about 70% of normal. By December 1 there was 48 inches of snow at the Tebay aerial marker and 12 inches at Notch Airstrip marker in the upper Chitina River. The data from the early season surveys showed the Basin Floor at 135% of normal, the Chugach Range at 134% of normal, and the Wrangell Mountains at 113% of normal.

For the March 1 surveys the snow depths and snow water contents were above average to well above average. The Wrangell Mountain snow courses were 124% of normal, the Chugach Range sites were 141% of normal, and the Basin Floor was 128 % of normal. The Long Glacier aerial marker had 28 inches of snow on March 1 and Notch Airstrip had 18 inches of snow. The marker at Tebay showed 100 inches of snow with a water content of 30.0 inches. The above normal conditions persisted into April with snow depths ranging from 21 inches in the eastern area of WRST at Notch, to 24 inches at May Creek. Long Glacier had 36 inches of snow on April 1 and Tebay had 93 inches. The Chokosna snow course along the McCarthy Road had 23 inches of snow and 5.2 inches of water content, normal is 22 inches of snow and 3.9 inches of water content.

There was no snow at May Creek on May 1 which is normal and no snow at most of the lower elevation snow courses in the area. The mountains still had snowpacks that were above normal. The Basin Floor was at 103% of normal for the last survey of the season. The Chugach Range was about 125% of normal and the Wrangell Range was 100% of normal. Figure 7 shows the NRCS snow survey report graphs for the area (NRCS, 2012).

The SNOTEL site at May Creek reported 5.2 inches of snow water equivalent on May 1st; the annual total precipitation was 14.0 inches, so the winter snowfall accounted for 37% of the total precipitation for the year. The snow-on date was October 18, 2011 and the snow-off date was April 27, 2012.

The Yakutat summary is included in this section because it helps characterize the north Gulf Coast and the southern extent of WRST. There are no snow courses in this area, but the NWS Yakutat COOP station records snowfall. It was an impressive year for the north Gulf Coast. The site reported a total of 326 inches of snow for the year, or 175% of the 185 inches the site normally receives. The snowfall total for January was 104.9 inches, normal is 34.6 and March snowfall total was 69.1 inches, while normal is 36.8 inches. October and April had very little snow accumulation. See Appendix C for graphs related to the Yakutat site.

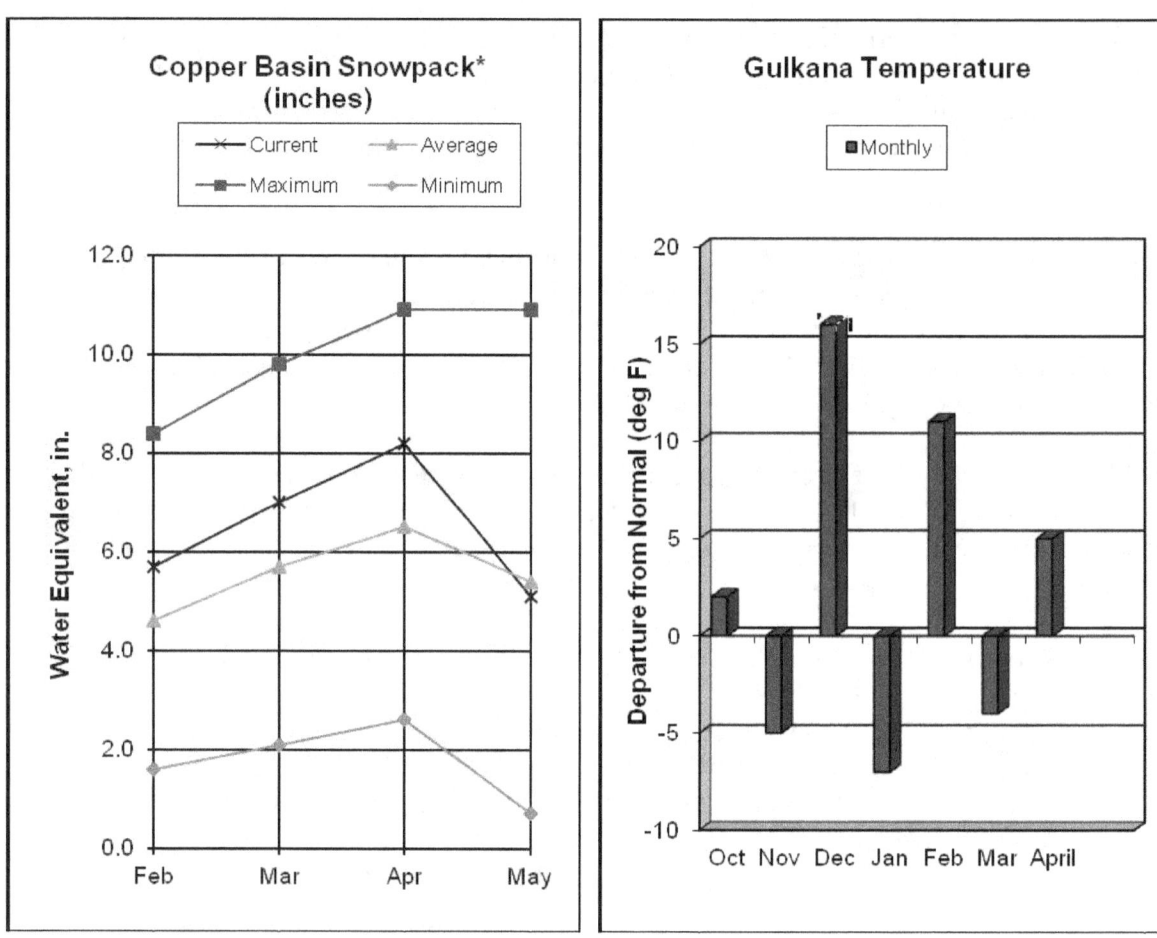

Figure 7. Copper Basin 2011-2012 snow season. Courtesy of NRCS, Anchorage, AK 2012.

Matanuska – Susitna Basin

According to the CAKN Tokositna Valley SNOTEL site, the first measurable snow that persisted through the winter appears to be around October 15, the exact date is difficult to determine because the snow depth sensor was measuring vegetation around the sensor up until the snow started falling. The December 1 survey of the aerial markers on the south side of the Alaska Range at Denali had snow depths that ranged from 9 inches at Chelatna Lake to 28 inches at Tokositna Valley. There were no surveys done on February 1 due to poor flying conditions, but the Tokositna Valley site reported 54 inches of snow with 12.5 inches of water content, normal is 55 inches and 13.6 inches of water content.

By March 1 most of the aerial markers were reporting snow depths and snow water contents that were above normal. The snow depth at Chelatna Lake was 59 inches, 140% of normal with 13.8 inches of water content. The Dutch Hill marker had 90 inches of snow and 23.8 inches of water content, 118% and 103% of normal respectively. The Tokositna site had 67 inches of snow on March 1, which is normal. There was some additional snow accumulation in April and the snowpack was just below normal by the April 1 snow survey. On May 1st the Tokositna Valley site had 39 inches of snow with 14.2 inches of water content, which is 83% of normal. The aerial markers were on average about 85% of normal. Nugget Bench had 31 inches of snow and the normal for this time of year is 46 inches. Dutch Hills had 69 inches of snow, normal is 74 inches and Chelatna Lake was above normal with 35 inches of snow, normal is 33 inches for the May 1 snow survey. Figure 8 shows the NRCS snow survey report graphs for the area.

The precipitation gage at Tokositna Valley recorded 24.6 inches of precipitation from October 1, 2010 through May 1, 2012. This is 41% of the total annual precipitation of 60.6 inches for the 2012 water year. See Appendix B for more information on the Tokositna SNOTEL data.

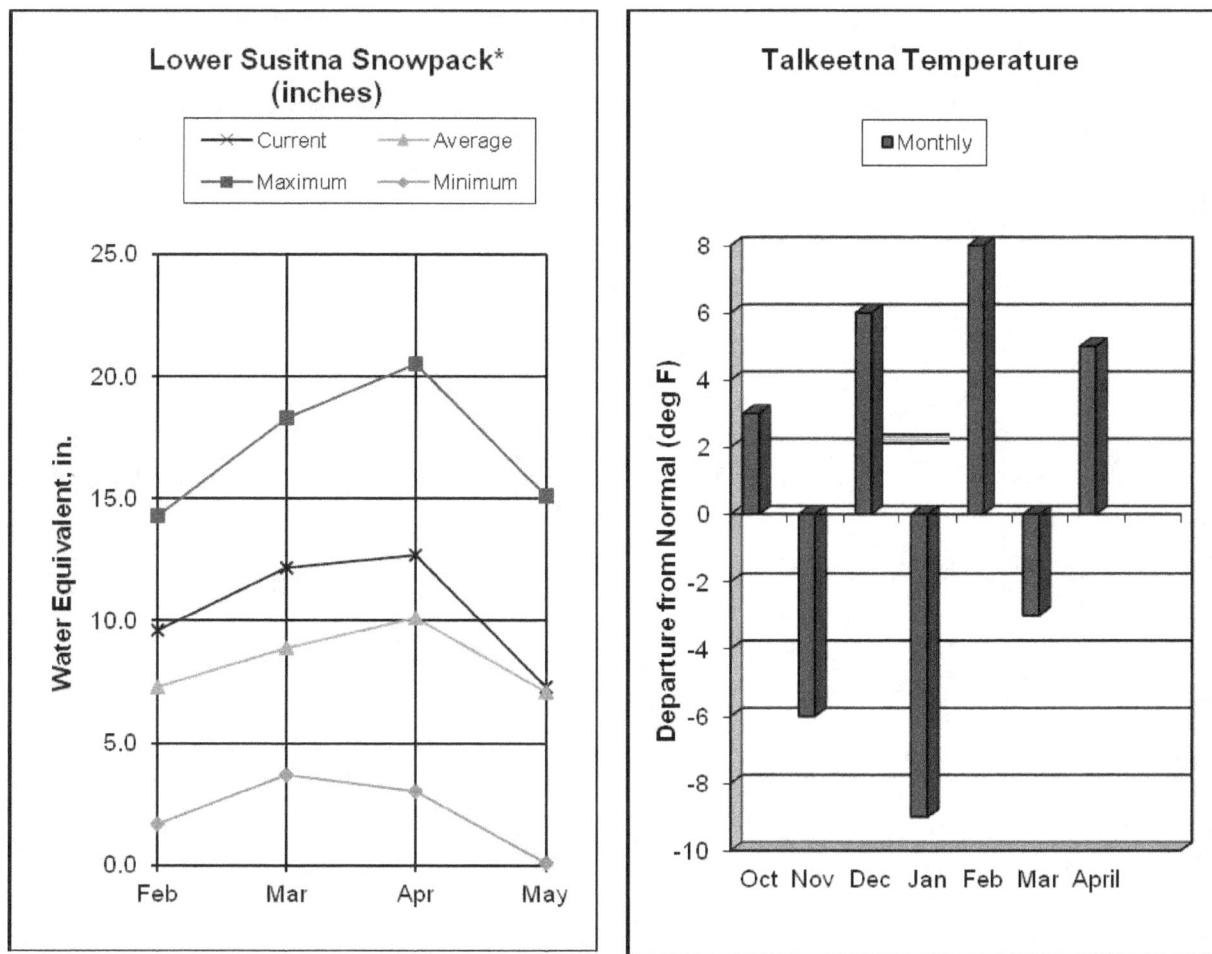

Figure 8. Lower Susitna Basin 2011-2012 snow season. Courtesy of NRCS, Anchorage, AK 2012.

Summary

There was an impressive amount of snow that fell in the 2011-2012 season in the southern areas of the state along the North Gulf Coast of Alaska which affected the southern regions of WRST, yet the snowpack for the central and eastern interior regions of the CAKN were at or just below normal, once again indicating that the snowpack across the Central Alaska Network was quite variable.

According to the NRCS, the central Yukon region, which includes Yukon-Charley Rivers, had snow conditions that were near normal. Long term records from Eagle show that site was just above normal. The upper Tanana Basin including the northern region of Wrangell-St. Elias was just below normal for the year. There were significant snowfall events in December and January, but little early or late season accumulations. The south side of the Alaska Range in the southern portions of Denali had above normal snow depths and water content for most of the season. The Wrangell Mountain Range in the central region of Wrangell-St. Elias and the Chugach Range both had snowpacks well above normal for the year. Temperatures in April were quite warm and the lower elevation sites, like May Creek, melted out. May temperatures however, were much cooler than normal, so any snow that persisted in the mountains through the end of April was still present through much of May and June. Yakutat, as well as most of the north Gulf Coast, as mentioned previously received an impressive amount of snow in the 2011-2012 season.

The NRCS publishes Alaska snowpack maps for each month the snow surveys are done starting on Feb 1. These maps give a nice overall picture of snowpack variability around the state (See Appendix E).

Literature Cited

Natural Resources Conservation Service (NRCS). 2012. Alaska snow survey report May 1, 2012. U.S. Department of Agriculture, Washington, D.C. Retrieved on October 16, 2012 from http://ambcs.org/pub/BasinRpt/2012/may.pdf.

Natural Resources Conservation Service (NRCS), 2012. Snowpack maps. Retrieved on October 16, 2012 from http://www.wcc.nrcs.usda.gov/cgibin/ak_snow.pl?state=alaska.

Sousanes, Pamela J. 2006. Snowpack Monitoring Protocols for the Central Alaska Network. National Park Service technical report, Denali Park, AK.

Western Regional Climate Center (WRCC). 2012. Climate data queries accessed on October 16, 2012 from http://www.wrcc.dri.edu/.

Appendix A. CAKN Snow Course Data from 2012

SNOW COURSE	ELEV.	FEB		MAR		APR		May	
Name	ft.	depth	swe	depth	swe	depth	swe	depth	swe
		in.	in.	in.	in.	in.	in.	in.	in.
Talkeetna	350	36	7.5	42	9.2	31	9.6	8	3.1
Tokositna Valley	850	54	12.5	67	15.7	58	16.3	39	14.2
Chelatna Lake	1450	***	***	59	13.8	50	14.0	35	13.0
Nugget Bench	2010	***	***	58	14.8	45	14.5	31	12.0
Ramsdyke Creek	22200	***	***	81	23.5	68	22.5	45	18.8
Dutch Hills	3100	***	***	90	23.8	69	25.0	69	27.0
Lake Minchumina	730	***	***	22	3.3	22	4.8	0	0
Kantishna	1550	21	4.2	24	4.7	23	5.1	5	1.7
Jatahmund Lake	2180	15	2.4	17	2.7	19	3.4	0	0
Rock Creek Bottom	2250	21	3.3	23	4.5	24	5.1	0	0
Rock Creek Ridge	2600	24	3.8	25	5.2	26	5.9	1	0.3
Lost Creek	3030	13	3.0	18	3.5	18	4.2		
Chisana	3320	15	2.7	18	3.0	18	3.6	6	1.7
Purkeypile Mine	2025			26	5.3	23	6.0	***	***
Tazlina	1225	21	4.8	22	4.5	22	4.8	0	0
Kenny Lake School	1300	21	4.1	22	4.7	23	5.2	0	0
Chokosna	1550	23	4.8	21	4.9	23	5.2		
May Creek	1610	23	3.6	23	4.4	24	4.8	0	0
Tsaina River	1750	56	15.3	69	20.0	65	21.6	43	18.4
Chistochina	1950	28	5.5	24	4.9	22	5.1	0	0
Tolsona Creek	2000	23	4.1	25	5.2	29	6.0	6	2.2
Dadina Lake	2160	28	5.2	43	8.0	33	8.5		
Sanford River	2280	25	4.8	29	5.2	29	6.0		
Long Glacier	4820	***	***	28	5.9	33	7.5		
Tebay Lake	1930	***	***	100	30.0	93	33.5		
Notch	2643	***	***	18	3.9	21	4.8		
American Creek	1050			18	3.0	21	4.0	8	1.6
Coal Creek	1000	***	***	20	3.2	20	3.9	***	***
Cathedral	1800	***	***	28	5.5	26	5.9	***	***
Copper Creek	2000	***	***	13	2.0	15	3.0	***	***
Crescent Creek	2600	***	***	18	2.8	22	4.3	***	***
Three Fingers	3350	***	***	27	5.3	28	6.3	***	***
Step Mountain	2850	***	***	30	6.0	30	7.0	***	***

*** = no report; blank space = no scheduled survey
Snow Course Averages 1971-2000

Snow Course Averages	1971-2000							
SNOW COURSE	ELEV.	FEB		MAR		APR		May	
Name	ft.	depth	swe	depth	swe	depth	swe	depth	swe
		in.	in.	in.	in.	in.	in.	in.	in.
Talkeetna	350	28	6.2	32	7.6	34	8.7	16	5.4
Tokositna Valley	850	55	13.6	67	15.7	62	18.7	43	17
Chelatna Lake	1450	36	8.3	42	10	44	11.6	33	10.9
Nugget Bench	2010	45	10.9	51	12.9	55	15.5	46	15.3
Ramsdyke Creek	2220	61	16.3	66	18.9	69	22	57	21.9
Dutch Hills	3100	69	19.6	76	23	80	27.5	74	28.7
Fairbanks Field Off.	450	21	3.5	23	4.1	23	4.5	3	0.8
Lake Minchumina	730	19	3.2	21	4	21	4.4	5	1.3
Kantishna	1550	26	4.5	28	5.3	30	5.7	15	3.1
Jatahmund Lake	2180	16	2.3	18	2.9	18	3.2		
Rock Creek Bottom	2250	20	3.7	22	4.2	22	4.3	8	2.2
Rock Creek Ridge	2600	24	4.3	26	4.9	26	5.3	14	4.9
Lost Creek	3030	25	4.8	26	4.8	21	4.2		***
Chisana	3320			22	3.4	22	3.6		
Purkeypile Mine	2025	20	3.9	21	4.2	21	4.1	10	2.5
Valdez	50	45	11.9	51	15.5	54	17.8	33	12.6
Tazlina	1225	17	3	20	3.7	19	4.2		
Kenny Lake School	1300	14	2.6	18	3.4	17	3.7	3	0.9
Chokosna	1550			21	3.2	22	3.9		
May Creek	1610			21	3.8	21	4.5		
Tsaina River	1650	50	12.5	56	15.7	57	17.6	41	14.6
Chistochina	1950	18	3	22	3.5	22	4.1	4	1.2
Tolsona Creek	2000	19	3.2	22	3.8	22	4.1	5	2.1
Dadina Lake	2160	24	4.1	29	5.1	27	5.9		
Sanford River	2280	24	4.2	28	5.4	28	6.2	15	4
Mission Creek	900	15	3.1	18	3.6	18	4.1	2	0.5
Upper Chena	3000	28	6.2	30	6.9	33	7.8	25	7.5

Blank space = record not long enough for normal calculation

Appendix B. SNOTEL Site Data

These data are available from the NRCS website and can be accessed at
http://www.ambcs.org/dbArchive.html and http://www.wcc.nrcs.usda.gov/

Kantishna: North Side Denali National Park and Preserve

Precipitation Accumulation – 2012 Water Year (Purple line)

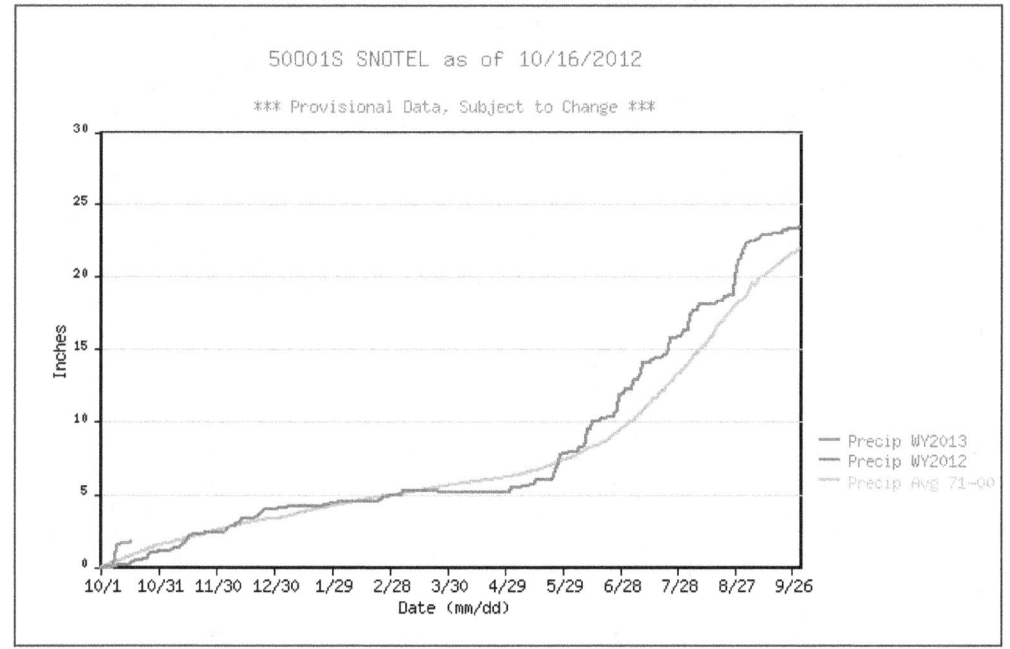

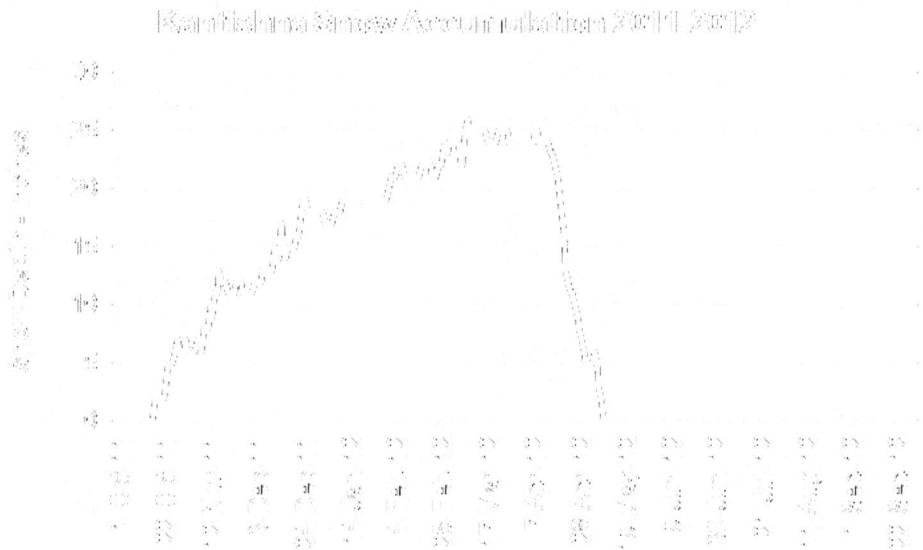

Daily precipitation totals for Kantishna for 2011-2012 season Oct 1 – Sep 30.
Unit = inches

day	oct	nov	dec	jan	feb	mar	apr	may	jun	jul	aug	sep
1	0.0	1.1	2.4	4.1	4.5	4.9	5.2	5.2	7.9	12.3	16.3	22.2
2	0.0	1.1	2.4	4.1	4.5	4.9	5.2	5.5	7.9	12.3	16.3	22.4
3	0.1	1.1	2.4	4.1	4.5	4.9	5.2	5.5	7.9	12.3	17.4	22.4
4	0.1	1.1	2.4	4.1	4.5	5.0	5.2	5.5	7.9	12.8	17.4	22.5
5	0.1	1.1	2.6	4.1	4.5	5.0	5.2	5.5	7.9	12.9	17.7	22.5
6	0.1	1.2	2.7	4.2	4.5	5.3	5.2	5.5	8.0	12.9	17.7	22.5
7	0.1	1.2	2.8	4.2	4.5	5.3	5.2	5.5	8.2	12.9	17.7	22.6
8	0.1	1.3	2.8	4.2	4.5	5.3	5.2	5.6	8.2	13.3	18.1	22.6
9	0.1	1.3	2.8	4.2	4.5	5.3	5.2	5.6	8.4	14.1	18.1	22.7
10	0.2	1.3	3.0	4.2	4.5	5.3	5.2	5.6	8.7	14.1	18.1	22.9
11	0.2	1.4	3.0	4.2	4.5	5.3	5.2	5.6	9.5	14.1	18.1	22.9
12	0.2	1.5	3.0	4.2	4.5	5.3	5.2	5.7	9.5	14.1	18.1	22.9
13	0.2	1.6	3.3	4.2	4.5	5.3	5.2	5.7	10.1	14.1	18.1	22.9
14	0.2	1.9	3.4	4.2	4.5	5.3	5.2	5.8	10.1	14.3	18.1	22.9
15	0.2	2.0	3.4	4.2	4.5	5.3	5.2	6.0	10.1	14.3	18.1	22.9
16	0.3	2.2	3.4	4.2	4.5	5.3	5.2	6.0	10.1	14.4	18.1	23.0
17	0.4	2.2	3.4	4.2	4.5	5.3	5.2	6.0	10.1	14.4	18.2	23.0
18	0.4	2.3	3.4	4.2	4.5	5.3	5.2	6.0	10.3	14.4	18.3	23.0
19	0.5	2.3	3.4	4.2	4.5	5.3	5.2	6.0	10.3	14.4	18.3	23.0
20	0.5	2.3	3.5	4.2	4.5	5.3	5.2	6.0	10.3	14.6	18.3	23.0
21	0.5	2.3	3.5	4.2	4.5	5.3	5.2	6.0	10.4	14.6	18.7	23.0
22	0.5	2.3	3.7	4.2	4.6	5.3	5.2	6.0	10.4	14.7	18.7	23.2
23	0.6	2.3	3.8	4.2	4.6	5.3	5.2	6.0	10.4	15.0	18.7	23.2
24	0.6	2.4	3.9	4.2	4.7	5.3	5.2	6.2	10.4	15.8	18.8	23.4
25	0.7	2.4	4.0	4.3	4.8	5.2	5.2	6.6	10.7	15.8	18.8	23.4
26	0.9	2.4	4.0	4.3	4.8	5.2	5.2	7.2	10.8	15.8	18.8	23.4
27	1.0	2.4	4.0	4.3	4.8	5.2	5.2	7.7	11.9	15.8	20.1	23.4
28	1.0	2.4	4.0	4.4	4.9	5.2	5.2	7.7	11.9	15.9	21.1	23.4
29	1.0	2.4	4.0	4.4	4.9	5.2	5.2	7.8	12.0	15.9	21.2	23.4
30	1.0	2.4	4.0	4.4	---	5.2	5.2	7.8	12.3	16.0	21.3	23.5
31	1.1	---	4.0	4.4	---	5.2	---	7.8	---	16.3	21.8	---
mean	0.4	1.8	3.3	4.2	4.6	5.2	5.2	6.1	9.8	14.3	18.5	22.9
max	1.1	2.4	4.0	4.4	4.9	5.3	5.2	7.8	12.3	16.3	21.8	23.5
min	0.0	1.1	2.4	4.1	4.5	4.9	5.2	5.2	7.9	12.3	16.3	22.2

Tokositna Valley: South Side of Denali National Park and Preserve

Precipitation Accumulation – 2012 Water Year (Purple line)

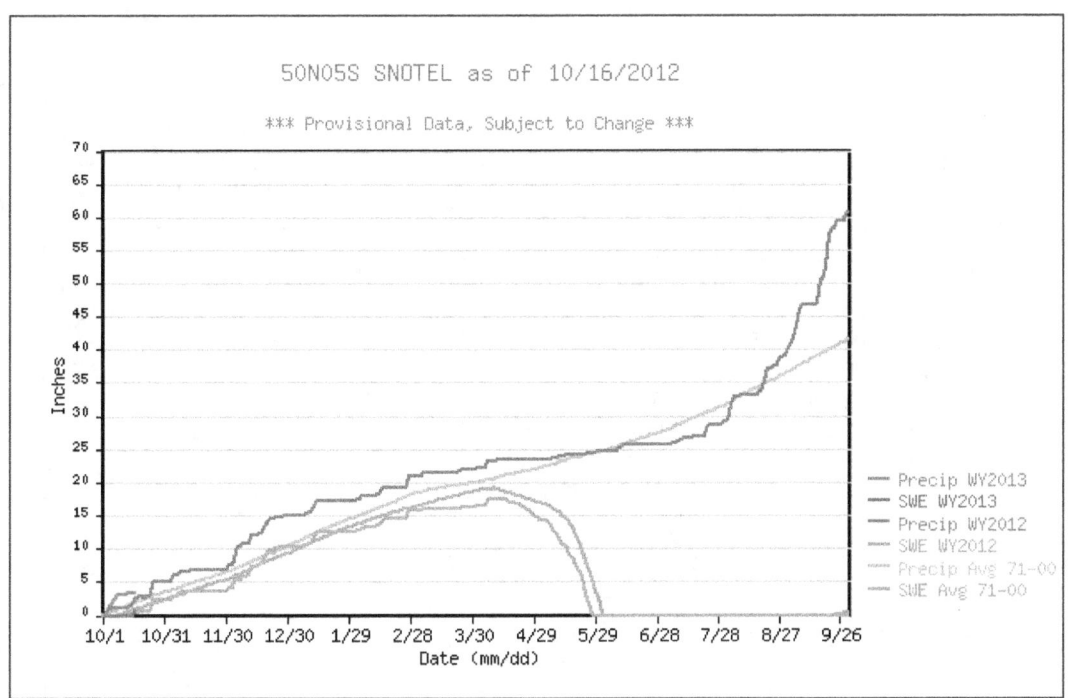

Daily precipitation totals for Tokositna Valley for 2011-2012 season Oct 1 – Sep 30.
Unit = inches

day	oct	nov	dec	jan	feb	mar	apr	may	jun	jul	aug	sep
1	0.0	5.2	7.5	15.0	17.2	21.0	22.2	23.4	24.6	25.8	29.2	40.8
2	0.1	5.2	7.6	15.0	17.5	21.0	22.2	23.4	24.6	25.8	29.8	41.1
3	0.8	5.2	7.6	15.0	17.6	21.0	22.2	23.4	24.6	25.7	32.0	41.8
4	0.8	5.8	8.4	15.0	17.9	21.0	22.2	23.4	24.6	25.8	32.1	42.6
5	0.8	6.0	10.3	15.0	17.9	21.0	22.3	23.4	24.7	25.9	32.9	43.6
6	1.0	6.1	10.3	15.0	17.9	21.5	23.1	23.5	24.7	25.9	32.9	46.0
7	1.2	6.4	10.3	15.0	17.9	21.5	23.3	23.5	24.7	25.9	33.0	46.4
8	1.2	6.5	10.7	15.2	17.9	21.5	23.3	23.6	24.7	26.2	33.1	46.7
9	1.2	6.5	10.8	15.5	17.9	21.5	23.3	23.7	25.2	26.5	33.1	46.7
10	1.2	6.6	10.8	15.5	17.9	21.5	23.3	23.7	25.3	26.5	33.1	46.8
11	1.2	6.7	10.9	15.8	18.1	21.5	23.4	23.9	25.4	26.7	33.1	46.8
12	1.2	6.7	12.0	16.6	18.2	21.5	23.4	23.9	25.7	26.7	33.1	46.9
13	1.2	6.8	12.1	17.2	18.5	21.5	23.4	24.0	25.8	26.7	33.1	46.9
14	1.3	6.8	12.1	17.2	19.0	21.5	23.4	24.1	25.8	26.7	33.1	46.9
15	1.9	6.8	12.1	17.2	19.2	21.5	23.4	24.2	25.8	26.8	33.1	47.1
16	2.1	6.8	12.3	17.2	19.3	21.5	23.4	24.2	25.8	26.9	33.1	48.9
17	2.6	6.8	12.4	17.2	19.3	21.5	23.4	24.2	25.8	26.9	33.6	50.5
18	2.7	6.8	13.0	17.2	19.3	21.5	23.4	24.2	25.8	26.9	33.6	50.6
19	2.8	6.8	13.7	17.2	19.3	21.5	23.4	24.3	25.8	26.9	34.2	52.2
20	2.7	6.8	13.8	17.2	19.3	21.5	23.4	24.3	25.8	26.9	36.2	54.9
21	2.8	6.8	14.3	17.2	19.3	21.5	23.4	24.3	25.8	27.0	37.1	57.2
22	2.7	6.8	14.5	17.2	19.3	21.5	23.4	24.2	25.8	28.2	37.1	57.9
23	2.8	6.8	14.6	17.2	19.3	21.6	23.4	24.2	25.8	28.4	37.1	58.1
24	3.1	6.8	14.7	17.2	19.3	21.8	23.4	24.2	25.8	28.7	37.5	59.0
25	4.6	6.8	14.7	17.2	19.3	21.9	23.4	24.4	25.8	28.7	37.6	59.4
26	5.0	6.8	14.8	17.2	19.4	21.9	23.4	24.4	25.8	28.7	37.6	59.4
27	5.1	6.8	14.8	17.2	21.0	21.9	23.4	24.4	25.8	28.7	38.7	59.4
28	5.1	6.8	15.0	17.2	21.0	22.0	23.4	24.4	25.8	28.7	38.9	59.4
29	5.1	6.8	15.0	17.2	21.0	22.0	23.4	24.5	25.8	28.7	39.0	60.5
30	5.1	6.8	15.0	17.2	---	22.0	23.4	24.6	25.8	28.8	39.0	60.6
31	5.2	---	15.0	17.2	---	22.0	---	24.6	---	29.2	39.5	---
mean	2.4	6.5	12.3	16.5	18.8	21.5	23.2	24.0	25.4	27.2	34.7	50.8
max	5.2	6.8	15.0	17.2	21.0	22.0	23.4	24.6	25.8	29.2	39.5	60.6
min	0.0	5.2	7.5	15.0	17.2	21.0	22.2	23.4	24.6	25.7	29.2	40.8

May Creek SNOTEL: Wrangell –St. Elias National Park and Preserve

Precipitation Accumulation – 2012 Water Year (Purple line)

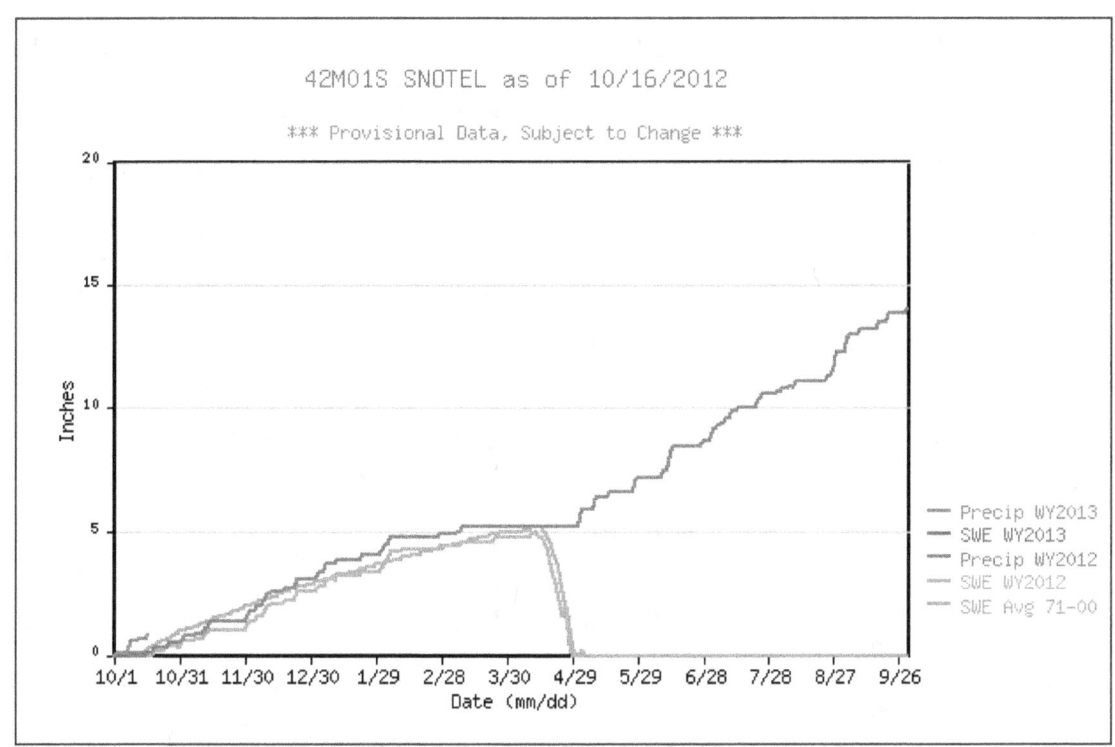

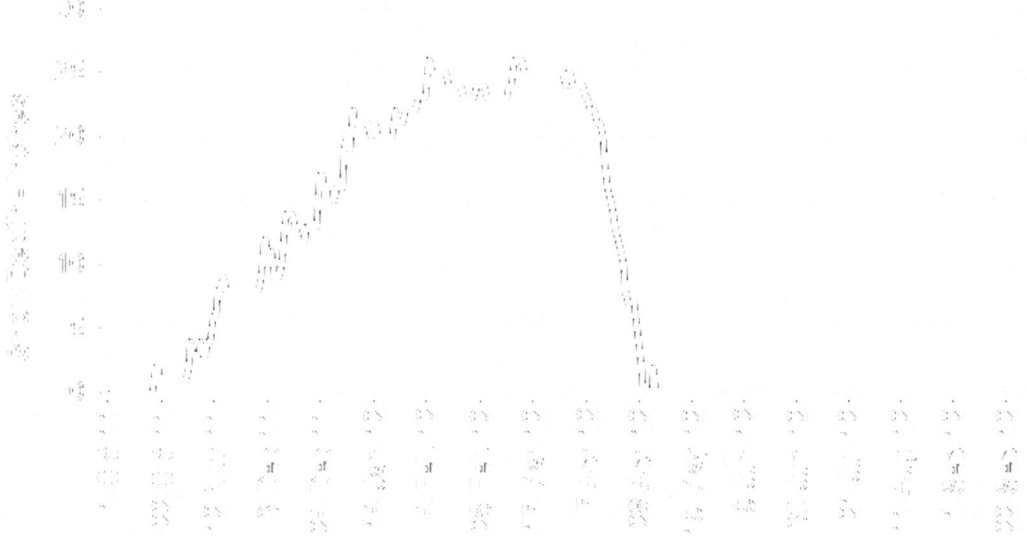

Daily precipitation totals for May Creek for 2011-2012 season Oct 1 – Sep 30.
Unit = inches

day	oct	nov	dec	jan	feb	mar	apr	may	jun	jul	aug	sep
1	0.0	0.7	1.7	3.1	4.3	4.9	5.2	5.2	7.2	8.8	10.7	12.3
2	0.0	0.8	1.8	3.3	4.4	4.9	5.2	5.5	7.2	9.2	10.7	12.9
3	0.0	0.8	1.8	3.4	4.5	4.9	5.2	5.9	7.2	9.2	10.8	12.9
4	0.0	0.8	1.8	3.4	4.8	4.9	5.2	5.9	7.2	9.3	10.8	13.0
5	0.0	0.8	2.0	3.6	4.8	4.9	5.2	5.9	7.2	9.3	10.8	13.0
6	0.1	0.8	2.0	3.7	4.8	4.9	5.2	5.9	7.2	9.4	10.8	13.0
7	0.1	0.9	2.0	3.7	4.8	5.0	5.2	5.9	7.2	9.4	10.9	13.0
8	0.1	0.9	2.1	3.7	4.8	5.0	5.2	5.9	7.2	9.6	10.8	13.1
9	0.1	0.9	2.4	3.7	4.8	5.2	5.2	6.4	7.5	9.6	11.0	13.2
10	0.1	0.9	2.5	3.7	4.8	5.2	5.2	6.4	7.5	9.6	11.1	13.2
11	0.1	1.1	2.5	3.9	4.8	5.2	5.2	6.4	7.5	9.9	11.1	13.2
12	0.1	1.1	2.6	3.9	4.8	5.2	5.2	6.4	8.2	9.9	11.1	13.2
13	0.1	1.3	2.6	3.9	4.8	5.2	5.2	6.4	8.4	9.9	11.1	13.2
14	0.1	1.4	2.6	3.9	4.8	5.2	5.2	6.4	8.5	10.0	11.1	13.2
15	0.1	1.4	2.6	3.9	4.8	5.2	5.2	6.5	8.5	10.0	11.1	13.2
16	0.1	1.4	2.6	3.9	4.8	5.2	5.2	6.6	8.5	10.0	11.1	13.2
17	0.1	1.4	2.6	3.9	4.8	5.2	5.2	6.6	8.5	10.0	11.1	13.5
18	0.1	1.4	2.7	3.9	4.8	5.2	5.2	6.6	8.5	10.0	11.1	13.5
19	0.3	1.4	2.7	3.9	4.8	5.2	5.2	6.6	8.5	10.0	11.1	13.5
20	0.3	1.4	2.7	3.9	4.8	5.2	5.2	6.6	8.5	10.0	11.1	13.5
21	0.3	1.4	2.7	3.9	4.8	5.2	5.2	6.6	8.5	10.0	11.1	13.7
22	0.3	1.4	2.7	4.1	4.8	5.2	5.2	6.6	8.5	10.0	11.1	13.9
23	0.3	1.4	3.1	4.1	4.8	5.2	5.2	6.6	8.5	10.3	11.1	13.9
24	0.3	1.4	3.1	4.1	4.8	5.2	5.2	6.6	8.5	10.4	11.3	13.9
25	0.3	1.4	3.1	4.1	4.8	5.2	5.2	6.6	8.5	10.6	11.3	13.9
26	0.5	1.4	3.1	4.1	4.8	5.2	5.2	6.6	8.5	10.6	11.4	13.9
27	0.5	1.4	3.1	4.1	4.9	5.2	5.2	7.0	8.6	10.6	11.5	13.9
28	0.5	1.4	3.1	4.1	4.9	5.2	5.2	7.1	8.7	10.6	12.3	13.9
29	0.5	1.4	3.1	4.1	4.9	5.2	5.2	7.2	8.7	10.6	12.3	13.9
30	0.5	1.4	3.1	4.1	---	5.2	5.2	7.2	8.7	10.6	12.3	14.0
31	0.5	---	3.1	4.2	---	5.2	---	7.2	---	10.6	12.3	---
mean	0.2	1.2	2.6	3.8	4.8	5.1	5.2	6.4	8.1	9.9	11.2	13.4
max	0.5	1.4	3.1	4.2	4.9	5.2	5.2	7.2	8.7	10.6	12.3	14.0
min	0.0	0.7	1.7	3.1	4.3	4.9	5.2	5.2	7.2	8.8	10.7	12.3

Chisana SNOTEL: Wrangell –St. Elias National Park and Preserve

Precipitation Accumulation – 2012 Water Year (Purple line)

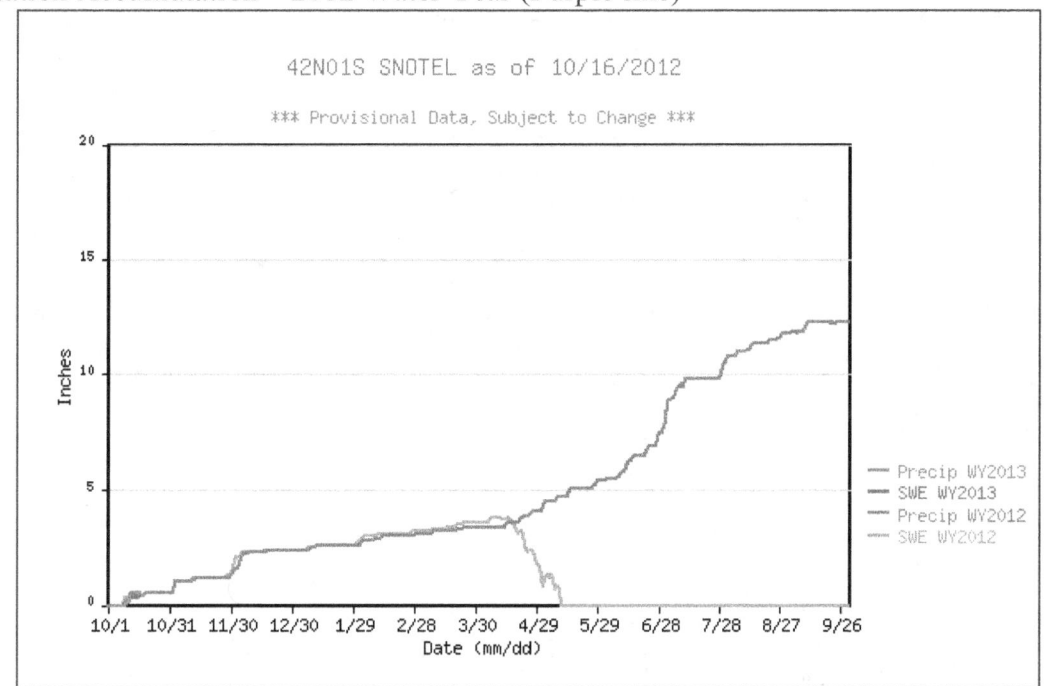

Daily precipitation totals for Chisana for 2011-2012 season Oct 1 – Sep 30.
Accumulated Precipitation - Since Oct. 1
Unit = inches

day	oct	nov	dec	jan	feb	mar	apr	may	jun	jul	aug	sep
1	0.0	0.5	1.5	2.4	2.6	3.1	3.4	4.1	5.4	8.0	10.8	11.8
2	0.0	1.0	1.6	2.4	2.7	3.1	3.4	4.2	5.4	8.8	10.8	11.9
3	0.0	1.0	1.6	2.4	2.8	3.1	3.4	4.5	5.5	8.9	10.8	11.9
4	0.0	1.0	1.8	2.4	2.8	3.1	3.4	4.5	5.5	9.0	10.8	11.9
5	0.0	1.0	2.2	2.4	2.8	3.1	3.4	4.5	5.5	9.0	10.8	11.8
6	0.0	1.0	2.2	2.4	2.8	3.1	3.4	4.5	5.5	9.1	11.0	11.9
7	0.0	1.0	2.2	2.4	2.8	3.1	3.4	4.5	5.5	9.4	11.0	11.9
8	0.0	1.0	2.2	2.5	2.9	3.1	3.4	4.5	5.6	9.5	11.0	11.9
9	0.2	1.0	2.3	2.5	2.9	3.2	3.4	4.7	5.7	9.6	11.0	12.1
10	0.2	1.0	2.3	2.5	2.9	3.2	3.4	4.7	5.8	9.5	11.0	12.3
11	0.2	1.1	2.3	2.6	2.9	3.2	3.4	4.7	5.8	9.8	11.1	12.3
12	0.3	1.1	2.3	2.6	3.0	3.2	3.4	4.7	6.2	9.8	11.2	12.3
13	0.4	1.2	2.3	2.6	3.0	3.2	3.4	4.7	6.3	9.8	11.3	12.3
14	0.4	1.2	2.3	2.6	3.0	3.2	3.5	4.7	6.3	9.8	11.4	12.3
15	0.4	1.2	2.3	2.6	3.0	3.2	3.6	5.0	6.4	9.8	11.4	12.3
16	0.4	1.2	2.3	2.6	3.0	3.2	3.6	5.1	6.5	9.8	11.4	12.3
17	0.4	1.2	2.3	2.6	3.0	3.2	3.6	5.1	6.5	9.8	11.4	12.3
18	0.4	1.2	2.4	2.6	3.0	3.2	3.6	5.1	6.5	9.8	11.4	12.3
19	0.5	1.2	2.4	2.6	3.0	3.2	3.6	5.1	6.5	9.8	11.4	12.3
20	0.5	1.2	2.4	2.6	3.0	3.2	3.6	5.1	6.5	9.8	11.4	12.3
21	0.5	1.2	2.4	2.6	3.0	3.3	3.8	5.1	6.7	9.8	11.4	12.2
22	0.5	1.2	2.4	2.6	3.0	3.3	3.8	5.1	6.8	9.8	11.5	12.3
23	0.5	1.2	2.4	2.6	3.0	3.3	3.9	5.1	6.9	9.8	11.5	12.2
24	0.5	1.2	2.4	2.6	3.0	3.4	3.9	5.1	6.9	9.8	11.5	12.3
25	0.5	1.2	2.4	2.6	3.0	3.4	3.9	5.1	6.9	9.8	11.5	12.3
26	0.5	1.2	2.4	2.6	3.0	3.4	4.0	5.1	6.9	9.8	11.6	12.3
27	0.5	1.2	2.4	2.6	3.0	3.4	4.1	5.2	7.2	9.8	11.6	12.3
28	0.5	1.2	2.4	2.6	3.0	3.4	4.1	5.2	7.5	9.8	11.8	12.3
29	0.5	1.2	2.4	2.6	3.1	3.4	4.1	5.4	7.5	10.3	11.8	12.3
30	0.5	1.3	2.4	2.6	---	3.4	4.1	5.4	7.8	10.5	11.8	12.3
31	0.5	---	2.4	2.6	---	3.4	---	5.4	---	10.5	11.8	---
mean	0.3	1.1	2.2	2.5	2.9	3.2	3.6	4.9	6.3	9.6	11.3	12.2
max	0.5	1.3	2.4	2.6	3.1	3.4	4.1	5.4	7.8	10.5	11.8	12.3
min	0.0	0.5	1.5	2.4	2.6	3.1	3.4	4.1	5.4	8.0	10.8	11.8

Appendix C. Long-term snowfall data – NWS COOP

These data are available courtesy of the Western Regional Climate Center web site at
http://www.wrcc.dri.edu

NWS COOP sites with monthly snowfall measurements
Note NWS calculates annual snowfall totals from July 1 – June 30.

Site (# of years)	Jul	Aug	Sep	Oct	Nov	Dec	Jan	Feb	Mar	Apr	May	Jun	Annual
McKinley Park (80)													
2011-12	0	0	2.6	5.5	12.2	18	14	10.3	5	0.6	1.3		**80.7**
Long-term Average	*0.0*	*0.0*	*3.5*	*12.7*	*13.0*	*12.5*	*11.6*	*9.8*	*8.0*	*6.1*	*2.3*	*0.2*	***79.6***
Eagle (31)													
2011-12	0.0	0.0	0.0	5.5	7.0	17.9	13.4	7.7	3.0	3.0	4.5	0.0	**62.0**
Long-term Average	*0.0*	*0.0*	*0.9*	*9.6*	*10.7*	*11.3*	*7.7*	*6.9*	*5.3*	*3.1*	*0.8*	*0.0*	***59.9***
Yakutat (50)													
2011-12	0.0	0.0	0.0	1.0	78.2	39.2	104.9	33.9	69.1	0	0.3	0.0	**325.6**
Long-term Average	*0.0*	*0.0*	*0.0*	*4.6*	*21.8*	*35.6*	*35.9*	*34.6*	*36.8*	*14.7*	*1.0*	*0.0*	***185.7***

Appendix D. Cumulative Snow Depths at CAKN Climate Stations

These data and additional graphs are available at http://www.wrcc.dri.edu/NPS.html.

Denali

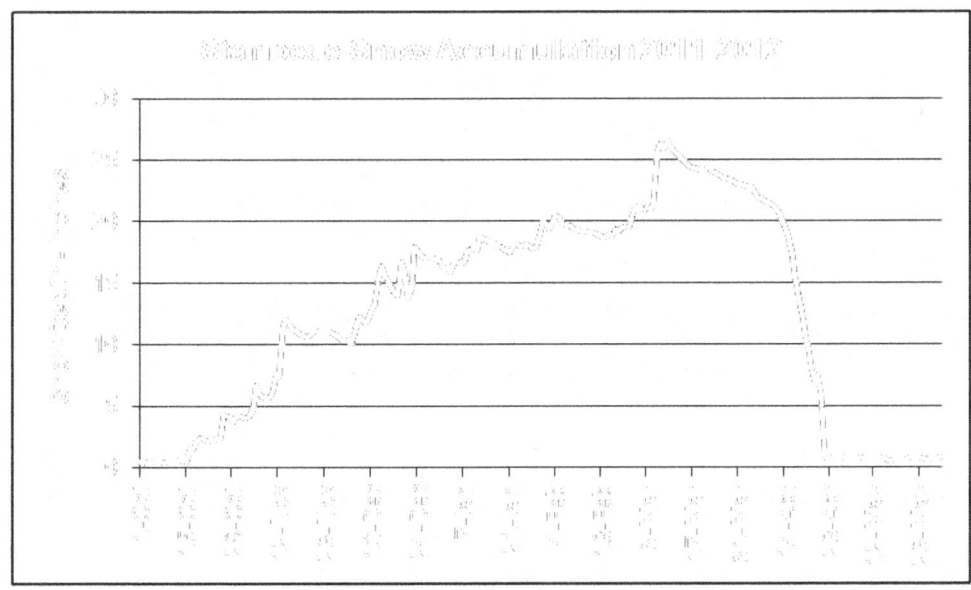

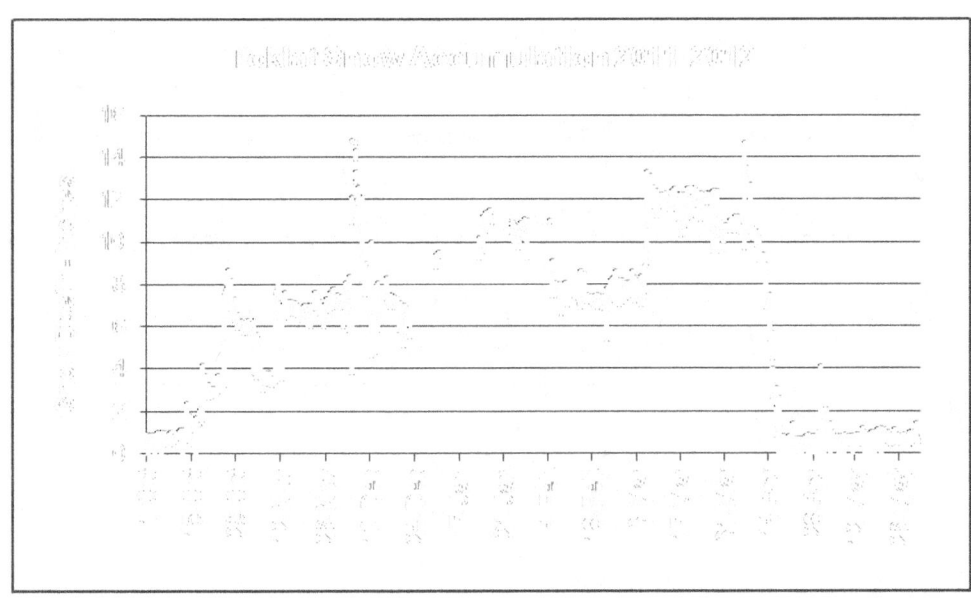

Wrangell – St. Elias

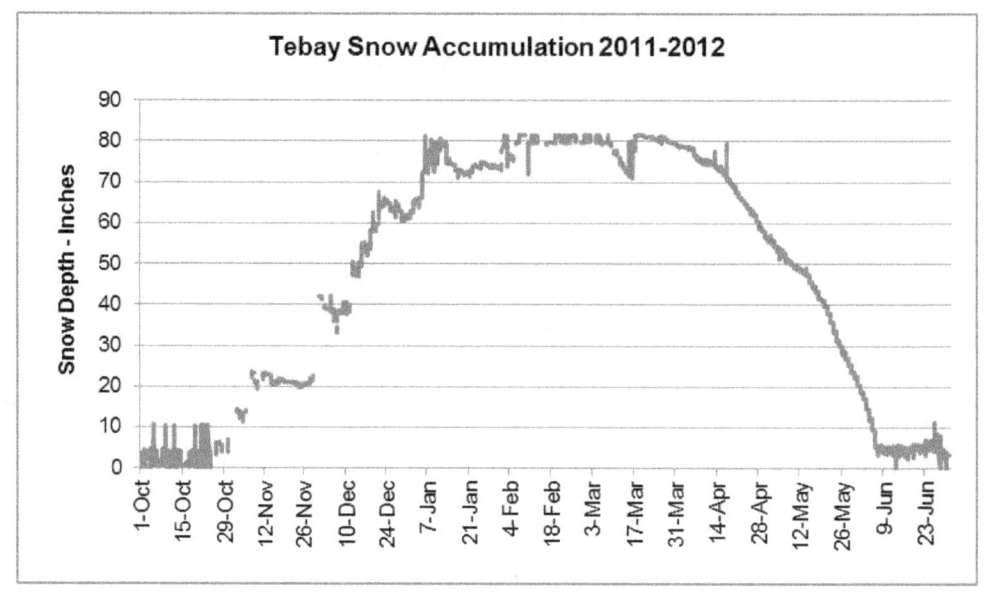

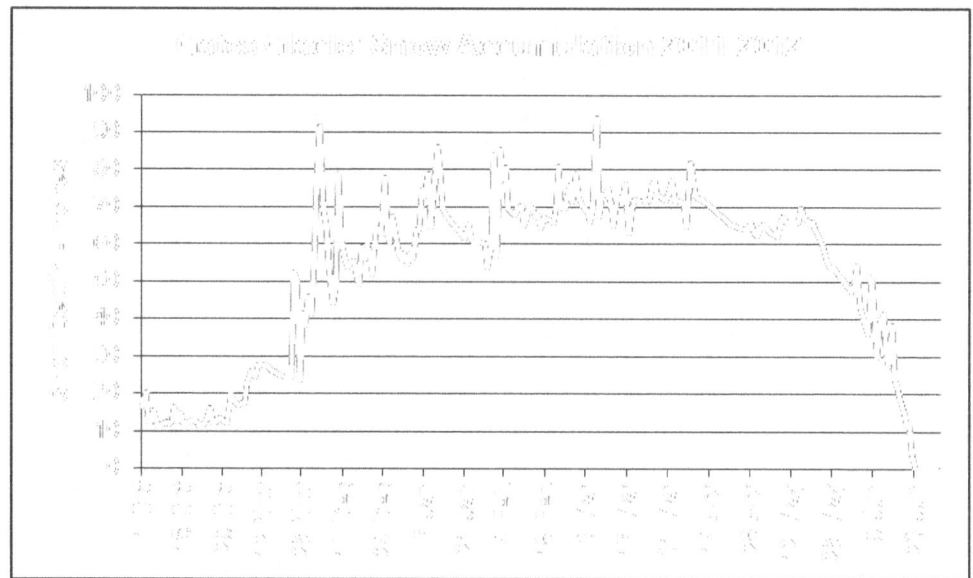

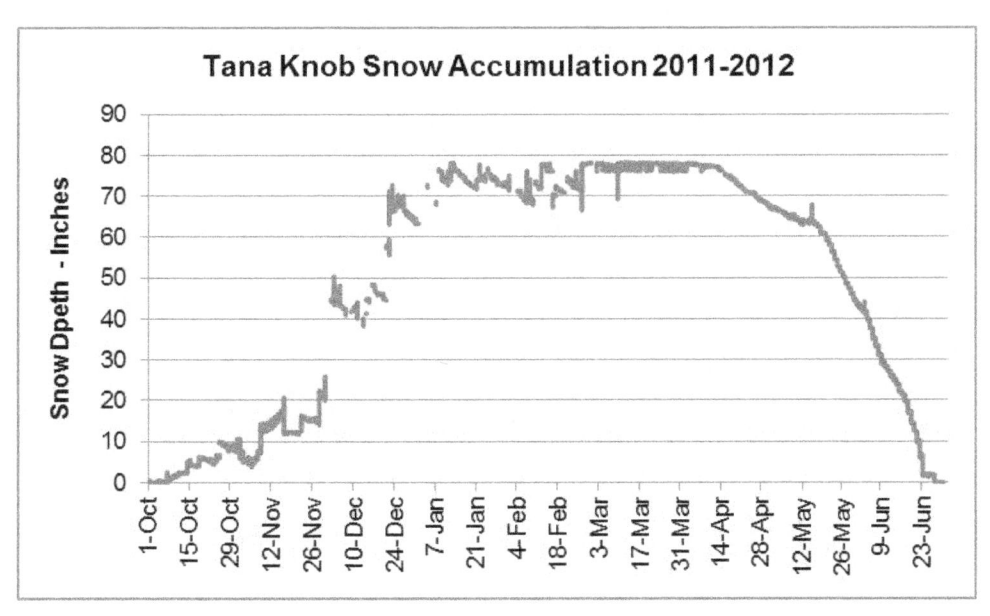

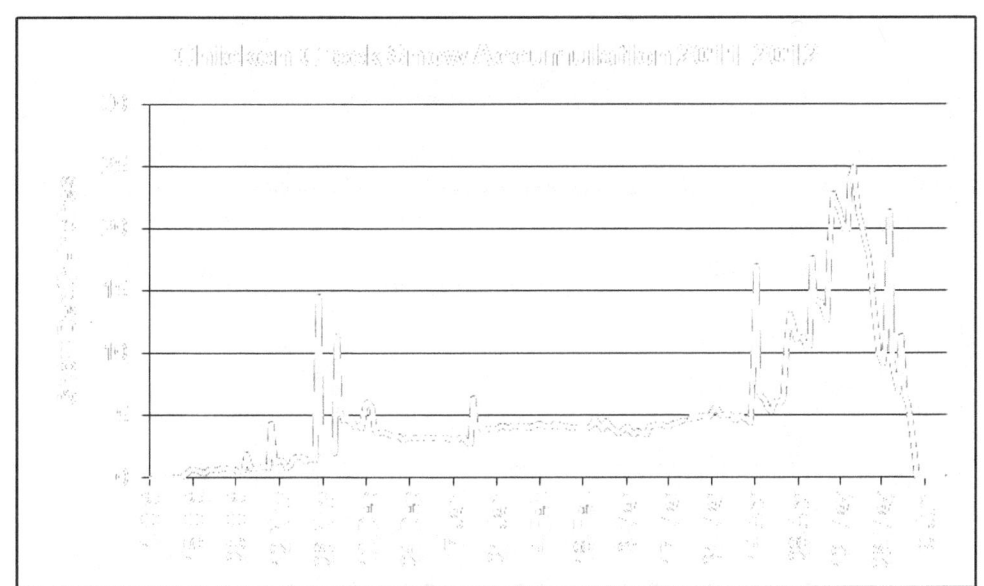

Yukon-Charley Rivers

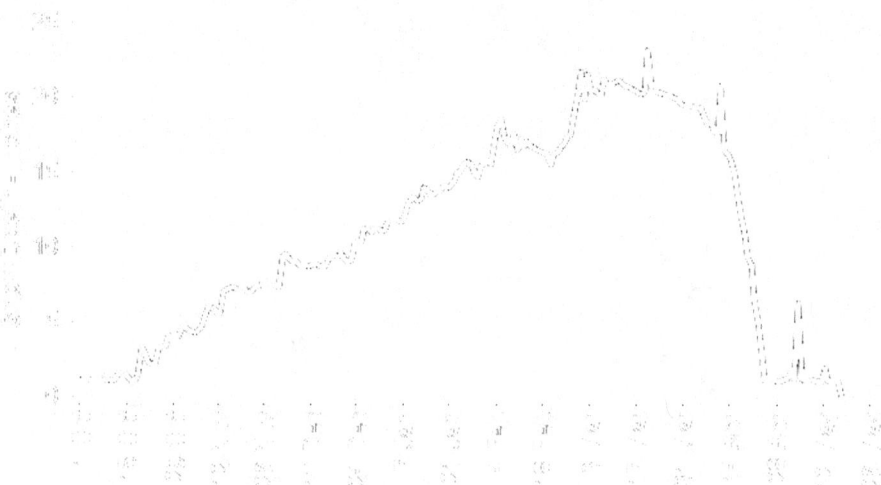

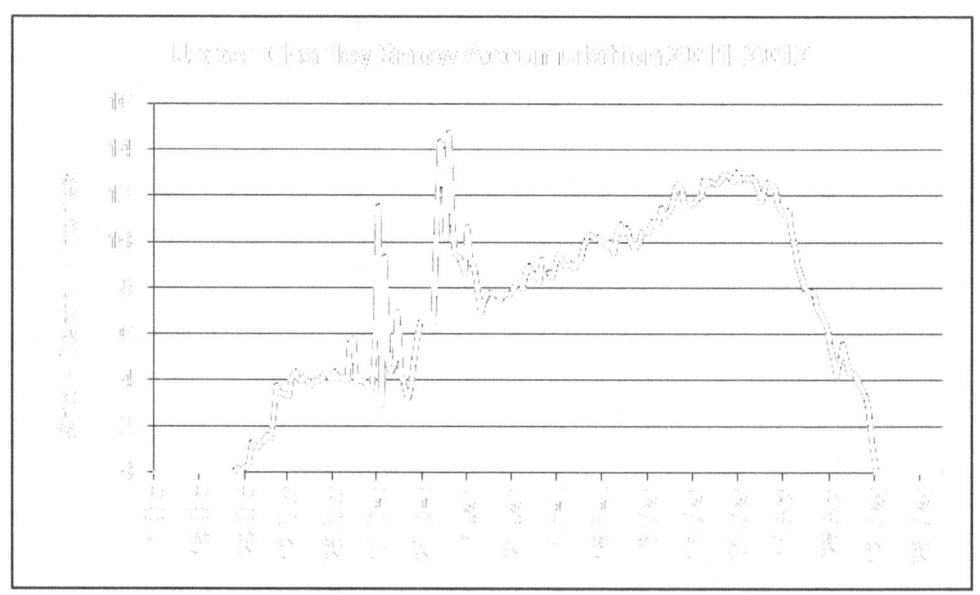

Appendix E. Statewide Snowpack Maps for 2011 - 2012

Published by the Natural Resources Conservation Service each month during the season and available online at http://www.wcc.nrcs.usda.gov/cgibin/ak_snow.pl?state=alaska

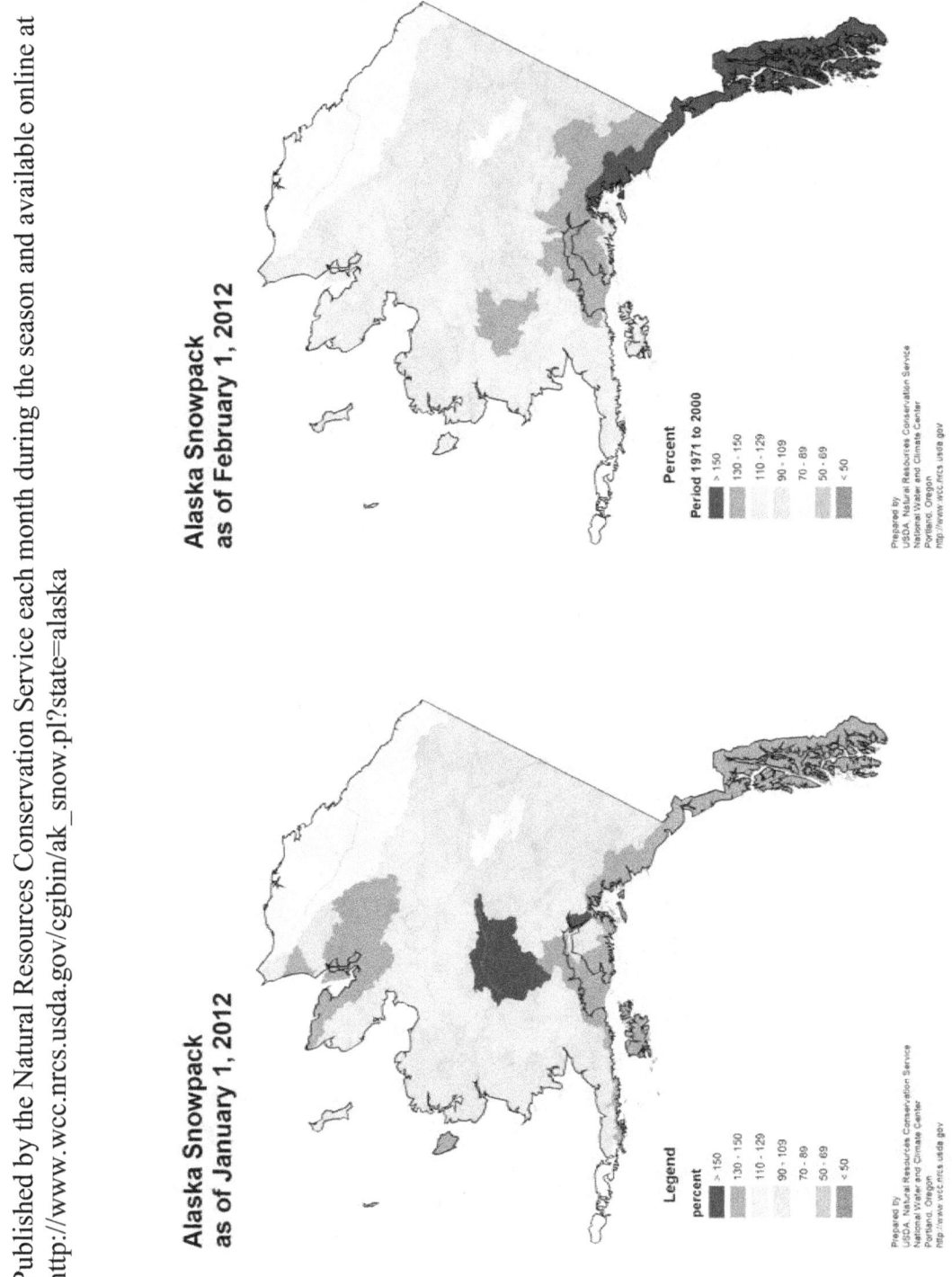

Alaska Snowpack
as of January 1, 2012

Legend

percent

> 150
130 - 150
110 - 129
90 - 109
70 - 89
50 - 69
< 50

Prepared by
USDA, Natural Resources Conservation Service
National Water and Climate Center
Portland, Oregon
http://www.wcc.nrcs.usda.gov

Alaska Snowpack
as of February 1, 2012

Percent

Period 1971 to 2000

> 150
130 - 150
110 - 129
90 - 109
70 - 89
50 - 69
< 50

Prepared by
USDA, Natural Resources Conservation Service
National Water and Climate Center
Portland, Oregon
http://www.wcc.nrcs.usda.gov

Alaska Snowpack
as of April 1, 2012

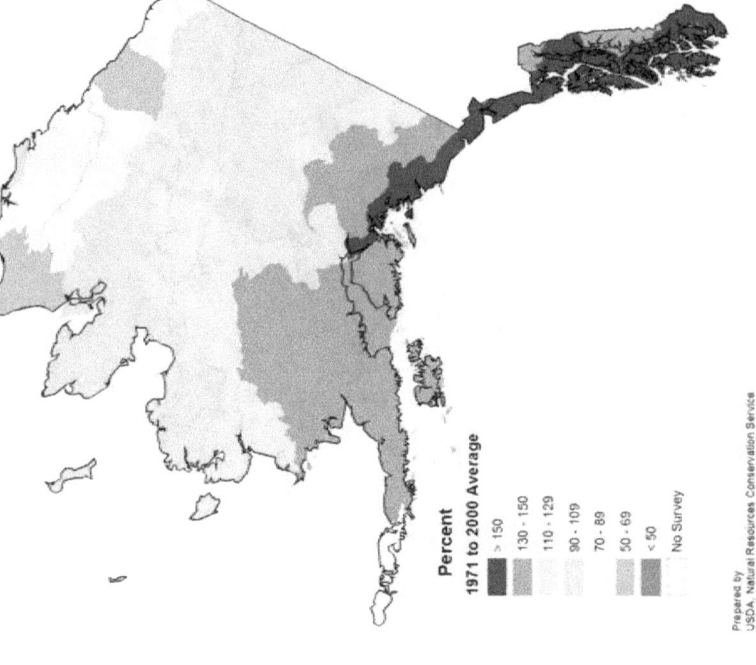

Percent
1971 to 2000 Average

> 150
130 - 150
110 - 129
90 - 109
70 - 89
50 - 69
< 50
No Survey

Prepared by
USDA, Natural Resources Conservation Service
National Water and Climate Center
Portland, Oregon
http://www.wcc.nrcs.usda.gov

Alaska Snowpack
as of March 1, 2012

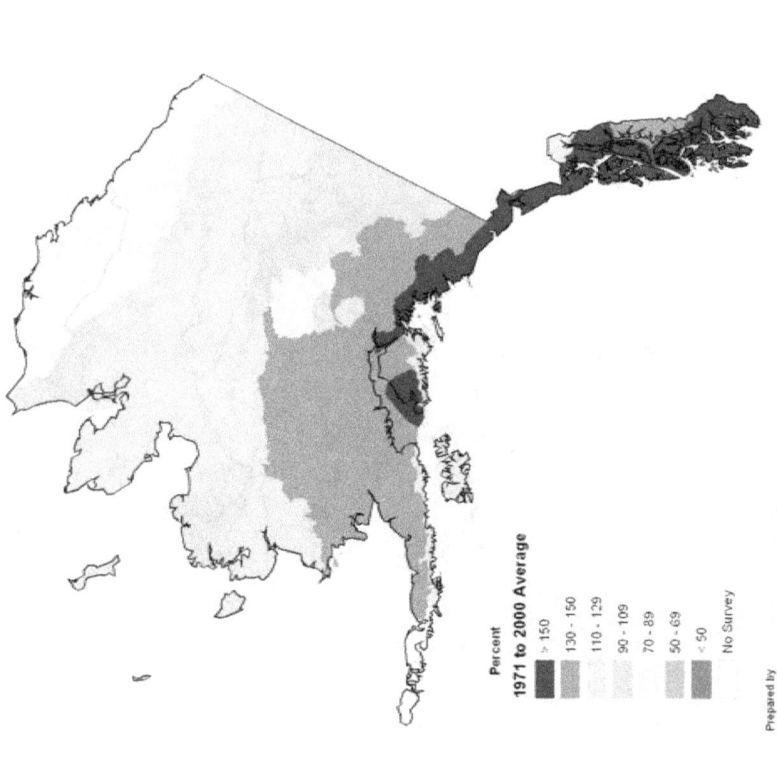

Percent
1971 to 2000 Average

> 150
130 - 150
110 - 129
90 - 109
70 - 89
50 - 69
< 50
No Survey

Prepared by
USDA, Natural Resources Conservation Service
National Water and Climate Center
Portland, Oregon
http://www.wcc.nrcs.usda.gov

**Alaska Snowpack
as of May 1, 2012**

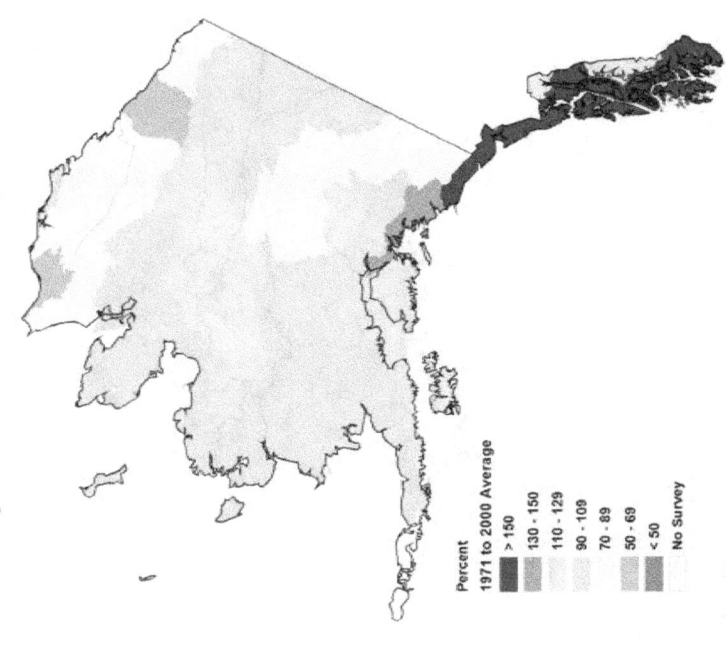

Percent
1971 to 2000 Average

> 150
130 - 150
110 - 129
90 - 109
70 - 89
50 - 69
< 50

No Survey

Prepared by
USDA, Natural Resources Conservation Service
National Water and Climate Center
Portland, Oregon
http://www.wcc.nrcs.usda.gov

33